Antler

JOHN CLEGG John Clegg grew up in Cambridge and currently lives in Durham, where he is completing a PhD on the Eastern European influence in contemporary poetry. A selection of his poetry was included in the *Salt Book of Younger Poets* (2010).

Antler

by

JOHN CLEGG

To John Greening
with all best wishes

28 / 8 / 13

S
SALT

CROMER

PUBLISHED BY SALT
12 Norwich Road, Cromer, Norfolk NR27 0AX

Salt Publishing 2012, 2013

Printed and bound in the United Kingdom by Lightning Source UK Ltd

Typeset in Paperback 9 / 13

ISBN 978 1 84471 964 8 paperback

1 3 5 7 9 8 6 4 2

for my sister

Contents

Acknowledgements

Some of these poems first appeared in the following publications: *Horizon Review, Succour, Pomegranate, New South* (Georgia), *The Grove, Toe Good Poetry, Mercy,* and on Dan Wyke's *Other Lives* website. 'Spell for an Orchard' was written for *Pocket Spellbook* (Sidekick Books 2010). 'Willow Tit' and 'Treecreeper' were written for *Birdbook Volume 1* (Sidekick Books 2011). 'Dill' was written for *Herbarium* (Capsule Press 2011). Some of these poems were previously published in the Silkworms Ink e-chapbook Advancer (2011). 'Pheasants' was published in *Silkworms Ink Chapbook 50*. 'Antler', 'Moss', 'Kayaks' and 'Luz' appeared in the *Salt Book of Younger Poets* (Salt 2011).

I am grateful to Jamie Baxter, Phil Brown, Alex Carruth, Maxime Dargaud-Fons, Alex Freer, Rowena Knight, Narayani Menon and Heather Yeung for their advice and encouragement. Particular thanks to Roddy Lumsden for his help editing this book, and Annick Sawala for her kindness and patience, both of which so far seem to be limitless.

Leather

Antler

This was the empire of antler,
walrus ivory, soapstone and marten furs;

this was a choked democracy
around a marketplace where local kings

of seven lakes or less demanded
garrisons; this was a trading post

where silverscrap and Arab coins
by weight changed hands for whalebone.

This is a town below the mud
where ninety graves so far have been

disturbed: soldiers on stools,
two children end to end, a seamstress

wrapped in leather, seal-
hunters, shamen, priests, and one

clutching a shinbone notched
in what is now an undeciphered language.

Moss

We feared the moss. We hollowed out
our ancestors and packed them with it,
left them smouldering in bark canoes.
On terminal moraines we blessed the moss
as herald of the thaw. Our children
got down on their knees to kiss it.
Kind moss insulated our pagodas,
bedlinened the herder on high pasture,
kindled grubby smoke for sacred visions.
We combed the moss. Our mosseries
were envied by the Emperor himself.
Spore cases, every size and colour, hung
like fireworks. We bred moss patiently,
too subtle work for human lifespans.
In the war we mulched the telegrams
demanding anaesthetic or poison moss.
Our holy valley stayed unoccupied.
Today, the only sound above a whisper
is the meal-gong. I meditate at night
on whether we are really growing moss.
Our mystics say the moss is growing us.

Piltdown

Your poems have to lie. I had a choice.
The skull I'd forked out half a fortune for
was worthless sarawak orangutan,
not caveman from the Downs: I'd been half-cut
on whiskey, paid in cash and woken up
to find it straw-wrapped in a packing crate,
receipt attached. A showman's pet
two hundred years old, maybe? Chips of gloss
were peeling off the cranium: a con,
a flimflam. I'd been made a mark

and though the man who sold it was long gone
I saw another way to get revenge.
The jawbone rattled loosely on its hinge
when I unhooked it, pried away the teeth
and dug through my display case for a vial
of fossil fangs: that was the turning point.
I laid them out like watchgears on black velvet,
pared the canines with a needle-file
and blunted the incisors. Grey dust shone.
Its human half came from the family vault.

Some folk believe that when God made the hills
he planted fossils as a test of faith.
That's not far wrong. The forger builds a world:
a present and a long past of his own.
The conman who fobbed off a monkey skull
on me had mentioned Piltdown. That was where
I picked to bring his artless lie to life,

to sculpt a kind of truth that would endure
from what he'd sold me, what I could flesh out.
I guess the lying art was in my bones.

Tributary Myth

I've never liked the thesis much
that there's a core of myth,
that every story we might tell's
a tributary off some main stem.

It relegates the details
to local colour: like the fact
it was a kayak, not a coracle,
stood empty in the lake's dead centre;

like the fact to us it would
have been October, and the man
was after salmon when he noticed
his reflection, beckoning,

and that he knew to reach and take
the outstretched hand would shatter it.
'A story told, with variations . . .'
But the story *is* the variation.

In some versions, he escapes.
In others, when he staggers back
weeks later, it's not him
returning, but the grey reflection.

The Whole Hog

was spit-roasted for writing sestinas.
A skewer through his intestines,
he parodied the insistence
of fire in an improvised sestina.
'Can somebody shut up the hog?' roared the Mayor.
His quick-witted personal assistant, Christina,
jammed an apple down the hog's throat.
Now the voice came burbling out of its backside,
improvising a lovesong to Christina
in flawless persona, as the Mayor!
Hoots rose from the crowd of hired yokels.

Everyone had some with applesauce.
Some smirking chefs presented me with the anus:
this, they assured me, was the 'best part'
and obligatory for visitors.
I scooped on extra applesauce.
It whispered to me 'Take care
I don't get lodged in your windpipe.
Recommend me to six of your friends.
I might get a poem from this, although I doubt it.'

Spell for an Orchard

Before the universe, there was the orchard.
The orchard is the universe's midpoint.
Each lost city was modelled on the orchard.
All myth and history started in the orchard.
Our apples banged the ground and that was thunder.
Our trees put down long roots and they were rivers.
Moss grew around the bark, and that was forest.

In the forest, two-legged insects chittered.
They sucked on sap and it was blossom honey.
They pared spears from torn splinters.
They saw a sparrow which they thought was God.
The real god is hidden in the orchard.
The rat behind the warehouse is the god of rats.
The wasp drowned in the barrel is the god of wasps.

The universe will not outlive the orchard.
The universe is larger than the orchard.
Larger is irrelevant. The orchard is better.
Our fruit dislodged the baby teeth of kings.
Our cider vinegar dissolved their crowns.
Our apples hang among the leaves like lanterns.
Now choose and twist. Each one is worth a world.

You dreamed that you were standing in the orchard.
Your lover said one word, and that was orchard.
You never found the right key for the orchard.
Your house lay just a little past the orchard.

You lay on moss, your legs spread, in the orchard.
You breathed the ripened air around the apple.
That brooch you lost, you lost it in the orchard.

Nightgrass

We led daygrass by the hand into grain,
found bread and beer there, the flail
and millstone in blueprint: so daygrass
and man were plaited together, altered
into a braid of cities along the delta.

Nightgrass was waiting outside folklore.
It spilt over stubblefields and burials,
nudged at the outskirts. Nobody bothered
to name it or notice, and quietly
a third colour wove itself into the braid.

Daygrass put forward her grain gods
to serve as ambassadors. Man agreed.
We'd tamed language with writing: now
we could use it to praise. But nightgrass
was thick in the cavity wall of the temple.

It tricked us with scarecrows who'd wait
till we'd turned round, then beckon the birds.
It got into everything. One autumn morning
we stumbled into the field like sleepwalkers,
and led grain by the hand into nightgrass.

A Dead Racehorse

An ancient flaw in an inch of metal
securing the horsebox onto the towbar
broke your back, but a deeper error
began your gallop in curb and bridle;
I've stuck up a poster next to the kettle
charting your evolution, each era
when every horse was a slow endurer.
I like best the one toward the middle

who grubbed for roots as the glaciers melted,
pigsize, toe jutting out at the shinbone.
You don't remember her rangy muscle,
how easily she'd have spooked and bolted
at storms. At least your death was sudden.
She died old. She left an astonishing fossil.

Folk Tale

As he rode through the forest he met a bear
who regurgitated the key to the city.

A man on a barge took the boy and his horse
twelve miles downstream; the boy

sat on his horse, the man sat on the prow
with a copper telescope, peering

toward the impending citadel, hoping
to catch a glimpse of the girl

doing star-jumps naked, bar a tiara,
he'd once either seen or dreamed he'd seen.

On his way home, having failed his quest,
the boy spilt a honeypot into his lap

and was eaten alive by a different bear
who also swallowed the key to the city.

This is the state of our ancient mythology
since the last of the gods lost interest.

Shaman Hunter

Out here a boy with a rifle
can crack the morning
a hundred miles in any direction.

He draws straight roads in the air
which swerve or veer
as they pass through the elk:

an artic jamming the brakes
too late, and watching
the shape in the wingmirror

sink to its front knees
then keel sideways. Nothing,
the boy believes, is an accident.

Even the thread of smoke from
the chamber is readable,
even the angle his cartridge spat out at,

the shallow light's scatter,
the blotch-tongues of lichen.
They all tell him to skin the elk.

Wounded Musk Ox

She keeps her half-pace,
shagged flank reddening
like sunset through thick fog,
her lunk brain failing
hours before her limbs.

Antler

An odd claw of bone
from the hub of the head,
once covered in velvet
and cabled with blood

now ossified utterly –
only the swerve
and feint of its grip
like a magnified nerve

to mark it organic.
It twists like a thought –
a petrified thicket
which broke in the rut.

Ramon Sije

after Miguel Hernendez

Leave me alone with just this grief
and grave and blank expanse of sky.
Your death's more real than my life.

I'm pinned up like a butterfly,
wings beating. Leave me. Let me work.
Of course no-one can tell me why

you didn't fight: a quiet jerk
on death's leash and along you went.
My own dog would have gone berserk.

I won't forgive that witty gent
upstairs, or Life and Death his goons,
or Earth his lapsed experiment.

I blow up storm-clouds like balloons
and axe-blades clatter at my feet.
Some orbit round my head as moons.

I'll eat his planet bite by bite
I'll flense the mantle from the core
I'll thresh the trees like they were wheat

if you don't speak. Our words before
are weightless now. You were a leaf.
Come back as wind. Break down the door.

Marimba Music

Here's the montage: skeletons trample an anthill,
a slit fish twitches on ice, the generalissimo
grinds his cigar-stub into a communist's belly.
Sparks rain on the foundry floor. Monsoon-rain
pings off the improvised mortar still hot
from a volley, and in the canyon revolutionaries
trigger a rockslide to buckle the train-track.

Turn down the radio's endless military waltzing
and let the marimba from nobody's quite sure where
provide a counterpoint for your inertia: this revolution
is made up and you know it. The dungeons
are not overflowing with carcasses, ringleaders
won't be hanged in the square later this evening.
And marimba chimes skedaddle down a back alley.

Las Perlitas, La Bicicletas, El Negro José.
I love the jittery bolero, its metal tang
the way air is supposed to taste after lightning.
Each struck note dissipates instantly, refines
the quiet around it: those tiny pops of silence
are seed-pods of the real revolution, red flower-buds
Miguel Hernendez coughed from his TB'ed lungs.

Petrified Forest

A polished cross-section of fossil tree
with a visible inch of borehole, gnawed
on the unfamiliar continent England was born from.

That burrow might be the one made thing
to last from whichever year it was worked.
As each flint axe in the upstairs collection

might be a whole tribe's sole memento
and stand for a vanished box of myth
or a vowelless language nothing remains of.

Each oil droplet carries, distilled,
the extinct, undreamt-for ancestors
of the capybara and modern horse, who lost their

chance of a name in the tectonic churn,
while this scrape on a tree was the one
safe place, swamped, turning from burrow to barrow.

Fly Embryo

At ten times life size
embryos swirl into focus:
frozen bootprints on a dirt road.

Cells have raised a shield-wall
along the border. Core to core
ciphers decode themselves,

a plume of chemical
communicates the land's lay.
This bulge is a future wingbud.

Still, the territory –
false tinted on the monitor –
is peaceful. Nothing stirs

as silently the real fly
extends into the Lebensraum,
its outline, its expanse of map.

Treecreeper

Bent apple
in the shadow of a cupola,

treecreeper
interrogating the trunk.

Spycatcher.
Pries open a wound in the bark,

dislodges
a spellbound mock-wasp

it bursts
with a jab to the back. Cataloguer

of hidey-holes
feathered with deadwood,

it knows
the caterpillar's schedule

and how to slip
over the border unnoticed

in winter.
It is nobody's national bird.

The Mysteries

In Rome's long autumn
I stole a jewelled phallus
from Cybele's temple.
History happened.
I drank from the Tiber,
throat slit by my fence:
a sleeper agent,
priestess in the Mysteries.

In tenement doorways
hushed conversations
pick round me carefully.
My corpse is crabmeat.
Dawn peers through keyholes,
rain turns leaves blood-coloured.
Luca my murderess
chiselled this tablet.

Kayaks

Our uncle in prison
sculpts bearpelts from soapstone,
tattooed his own shoulder:
a road-gang of caribou

gnawing the tundra,
the musk ox, the grey goose,
my brother and I
racing kayaks on meltwater.

The Balance

I took a slip-road off sleep's autobahn
and wound up on the disputed border.
They pressed record on the tape-recorder,
lit a cigarette and offered me one.
I asked if this was an interrogation.
Silently the patrolman underscored a
sentence: Travel permit not in order.
He left the pages underneath unshown.

I lied hard to him. Whatever he made
of my story, the barrier lifted,
the soldier leaning against it stepped
aside, and I woke up here afraid
that the balance had stirred or shifted
between the promise and the swelling debt.

Meteor

I was the brushstroke of light
above your orchard.

I was what the muntjacs found
at daybreak, and dragged turf over.

Then I was a spasm underground.
Roots sucked at my wellspring.

When your wife, still mourning
her firstborn, stepped out

among the apple-rows,
I was what watched

from the eye of a clipped branch,
from the eye on the arse of an apple.

I was the comet blood
in your cider keg, I was the sweat

which boiled off your drunk stupor.
I felt your wife press her face

in that pillow to taste me.
And I was the catch in her throat,

your lost estate, the inheritance
shared between no one and no one.

Monolith

The perfect wardrobe, hand-tooled,
unaffordable, dark innards
rippling with vicuna and merino

overlooked, hunched in a patch
of shade, a standing stone
he made love at the foot of.

He saw it as his Old Retainer,
straight-grained, drily jovial,
when really it was his Hollow God.

Inanna

The Underworld was worse than I remembered.
We lay on our backs and through thin reeds
we'd eavesdrop on the living. Barmen, clergy
and a spiderweb variety of fungus
were the only things to thrive. And bats
as well, grey nasty ones, our ancestors.

I'd ventured down on profitable business.
Factional infighting and bureaucracy
had choked my hope like knotweed (that
was something else which grew there).
Anyway, like most of the inhabitants
after a while, I drifted to a dive bar

where I might have drained to shadow. Then
one day there was commotion in the alleys.
Pushing through the crowd I saw Inanna
higher than a house and striding naked
to the Bull of Heaven's funeral.
She smiled at me. I heard a lion roaring:

it was new breath flooding through my
lungs, the elevator tearing upward
and the huge sea I'd been beached against.
I headed back to Uruk through the desert.
Since then, I've dealt in lapis lazuli
and turn a tidy profit, but never sleep.

Paul's Job

My job's not to talk about Paul's job.
I sit in the pickup and think about something else.
On my expenses I claim tobacco and paperbacks.

My job is the desert I have to oversee
and Paul's job is the sun I can't stare into.
Our pickup, thank god, is always and only our pickup.

A skeletal kangaroo draped on a crater's edge,
a stick-figure moving jerkily over the ridge cusp,
two distraction birds perched in a lancewood acacia:

this is what keeps my mind from fixing on Paul's job.
We have one CD in the truck we play till it skips,
Liz Phair's *Exile in Guyville*; last year

it was *Diamonds and Rust* by Joan Baez.
Both speakers are heat-warped. Joan's strum and words
have set crystal in me, frozen to mantra

I can repeat when otherwise I'd think of Paul's job.
My buttocks have dug an inverse arse in the truckseat,
a spit-gob cooks on the bonnet and Paul

is striding toward me through the red.
Scraping mud on the step's corrugation, he gestures
for me to rev the engine and hit the B-road

we'll shudder along for hours in silence, him eyeing
his fingertips while I plough the career
I've planted, not mentioning Paul's job.

Wildfire

for Jamie Baxter

It finishes. Rain's million aimless kisses
soothe ash into rivulets, and lift
the smoke over a grove of emptinesses:
dark hollows on a cliff, but no cliff left.

Luz

Another body brought to me. I root
redhanded through the lights and cooling meat

and every bone I dredge I plunge in brine
as if it was a paintbrush. Flexing fine-

tipped jeweller's pliers in the corpse
I snag the earbones, hammer, anvil, stirrups,

each smaller than my smallest fingernail.
The bone I'm looking for is smaller still.

No pounder crushes it, no earthly fire
raises down its length one hint of char.

Leave it to marinate in fluoric acid
and it won't dissolve. Joachim Hachasid

claims it as the last bone in the spine.
Vesalius labels this the *Juden Knöchlein*:

jew-bone or resurrection bone or *luz*,
the almond out of which the body grows

again on Judgement Day. I scour and scour
for the tiny seed, the tight-packed flower.

Wisdom Literature

Concentrate yourself against subjects who prove non-existent,
in whose respect no faith can be placed!
Do not approach them when you are alone!

– from The Teachings of King Amenemhat

Sorrows of waterfowl | outweigh the rainfall.

I woke sore-headed | and covered in hieroglyphs.

Splayed on a tripod, | the Oracle defecates.

Stone Ozymandias | now on its last legs.

Who was the Moon God? | Best check Wikipedia.

Crack in the casket; | papyri expiring.

Under the mummy-cloth, | King, are you naked?

Odd omen: a bright bird | taking off backward.

Lace

Mermaids

We'd explode from the change in pressure
before we saw daylight, and anyway
evolution has sheathed our eyes as dead ends.
We live by taste, which is really smell;
we taste what's diffused in water
and sense the direction. Carcasses mostly.

We've kept a vague idea of our shape:
wing-spindles propelling us forward,
armoured backplate, excretory organs.
But sex is a mystery. Our best guess
has males as the krill-like specks
which winkle, sometimes, under our chitin.

We sing to each other in pheromone, never
certain how message matches to sender.
Sometimes we taste our long past's echo.
We cultivate theories on the existence
of dry land, spin theologies of loneliness. We hang
translucent in love's deepwater trenches.

Purgatorio

Scrub tundra birthmarked
by a lone cloud-shadow
and a single road whose
parallel is the horizon.

I would say no traffic,
but this place is honesty
embodied, so: one bus
a fortnight, rarer cars

roofracked with skidoos,
and my rig, which passes
two small towns in eighteen
hours, hauling canned fish.

I've heard truckstop
stories of this route –
the UFO, the hitcher
beardless, weeks from anywhere –

and tell one of my own:
when my truck stalled
and froze, and how the road
scrolled underneath regardless.

Dill

Weighed down by last night's rain, it sprawls
and overflows the terracotta

leaving one half globe of knots
erect, its seedclutch, swaying dangerously.

Letting the filigree trail
against my palm, I cut handfuls for garnish,

each strand a traced blood vein,
a web of backroads pencilled into the mapbook.

The Empty Bottle

after Omar Khayyam

I

Our priests and prophets try to second-guess
the riddle: what lies *under* the abyss?
Don't waste your breath disputing them, my friend:
the one forgiving creed is drunkenness.

II

We last no longer than the spurt of spark
which lit the fire, no longer than the arc
our sun is tracing round one hemisphere.
An empty bottle overflows with dark.

III

There's someone you just were who can't return.
The sum of loss is nobody's concern,
not even yours. A million husked selves
have aggregated, raised you like a cairn.

IV

An empty bottle is a gaping mouth,
gums, windpipe, lung, a single long-held breath
without a tongue to twist it into words.
Baked somewhere in the glass are jagged teeth.

Seasons in the Frame Shop

I work in the frame shop that uses willow.
Different frame shops use different woods
which each have their strengths and weaknesses:
pine is especially cheap, balsa is pliant,
cedar– and sandal-wood frames can differentiate
photos of wives from photos of mistresses.
Willow is used for abstract art and found objects.
I suffered as a child from epileptic seizures
which left me with an aversion to abstract art;
nevertheless I do as good a job on the frames
as I can. I love willow. I wouldn't frame
with anything else if I was given the choice.
I tune my hand in calibration with the grain,
if I touch an inch of willow-branch I could tell you
the shape of the tree and all its faultlines
which serve to make the individual frame unique.
My shop's on a quiet sub-alley; days or more
pass without custom, my grin in all the mirrors.
When I carve willow, I'm the end of the world.

Theology

ICE FISHING

The ones I raise who see the light
for longest wind up on the grill.
I let half go. Should they survive
the shock of swapping elements

they might turn prophets of their kind
and spread the word, if they could find
disciples in the dark. Dark falls.
I walk on water with my catch.

LILITH

A minor angel catching up
on paperwork found Lilith's name:
she'd missed the apple and remained
both human and unfallen. So

the King of Heaven had her turned
into a screech owl. Now she bucks
across the sky tugging a sheet
of dark. The black winds bugger her.

Glaciology

Calving

The glacier is handing out
blank business cards, snout nuzzling
the sea: squashed ground exhales, dooms
the aurochs and the sabretooth.

Bergs tear. It could be this was when
the pale thought of early man
broke into polysyllables,
and consciousness began to thaw.

Tarn

Although it ploughed the moor and coaxed
the valley open, no-one turned
the glacier into a god.
We thought its timescale marked the edge

of our intelligible: then
in two lifespans it fled the village,
buried itself on the mountain,
white wall unseen in the black lake.

Lure

I named my pub after the local epic,
'The Marriage of Woodlouse and Flea'.
The village menfolk would bundle in
to bitch over kvass or woodchip liquor
until their wives came to haul them out,
which saved the expense of a doorman.
I kept it all to bribe the inspector.

In my first week, somebody told me
how to catch reindeer: their eyesight
so blurry a herder with arms raised
might be mistaken for a mate's antlers.
Your buddy crept up behind to net it.
I never saw a successful attempt.
In the meantime, government quotas

were separating the ancient herds.
I took a husband among the elders
who'd built a religion out of gossip.
On New Year's Eve we ate rancid butter
and let hot wax trickle over well-water
to see the future, which held its arms out
mimicking antlers, willing the beckon.

The King of Herring

for Helen Sims-Williams

You see him once at most, hauling the scoop
your net took from a shoal into the hatch,
or guess at him from sonar's phantom-sweep.
The smashed reflection writhing in a sack
resolves itself into a single fish, the sun
minutely shifts and hangs in every scale.
For a stretch he burns as clear as vodka.
Then the crane jolts, shows the real catch.

I've heard it argued everything we dredge
is slivers of him, that we eat his edges,
that his name's what choked fish gulp towards.
I've known men worry at him like a wound
or swear against their eyes under a hood
of steam in someone's sauna, drowned in aquavit.
Others would say he's not the herring king
but ours, and that his myth's a net to trawl him.

Willow Tit

Her beak is a split thorn
carving a zipline,
undressing the seedpod.

Ignore her calls,
those sudden shudders
of breath in a pinetree.

Ignore her completely.
Some birds in China
sculpt nests from spit;

she'll hammer a home
in your huge neglect,
eyeshadowed, black-capped.

In the land of the dead
the judges will balance
your heart and her feather.

Vaisala and Sinuhe

Imagine grinding a lens Leonardo's spreadeagled man
could slide comfortably onto,
the size you'd need to spot asteroids
from the 1930s and not confuse them
with regular scratches and nicks

on old photographs. Hold that picture.
Vaisala the Finnish astronomer
knew about lenses
till 1971: after which
radio silence.

Banks of telescopes under a midnight sun.
Da Vinci making an angel in the snow.
Imagine grinding a lens
which would render the photo lifesize.

II

It rains developer fluid.
Asteroids miss the earth by a million miles
and don't affect our destiny in the slightest.
He gives them important names:
Carelia, Donnera, Aino, Aura.

Icebergs in space
and Vaisala the only hand on deck.
He pulls himself out from under the lens

and starts on his stack of marking.
Notice the trance.

The charts on his desk
map constellations unknown to shamen
who navigate, he's sure, by the sound of stars.
Also a receipt for three blue shirts.

III

Vaisala's three patents
will make his brother the richest Finn
on the Forbes list, twenty years later.
The Nazis are winning in Europe.
Vaisala's gloved hand

is reaching across an enormous lens
to take another gloved hand
and it's hard to say whether
the flecks are glass dust or snow
or even ash:

the glow in the photo's left-hand corner
could be firebombs
or, indeed, aurora borealis.
Everyone is in everything up to their necks.

IV

Infatuated, Vaisala struggles to piss
in the forest. The Observatory's single toilet
is newly decreed a Ladies.
One night, he sees a track of pawprints –
fox, he decides, not wolf – which ends in a clearing.

The girl is off-limits,
a sepia postdoc from Turku.
Coming in from the woods weeks later
he reaches to grasp her hand over the lens;
outside in the rain-barrel,

he'd missed a sparrow whose guts
had unravelled and frozen. A bird-Alexander
might cut the knot, a tiny Theseus
thrash out a path to the heart of the matter.

V

He doesn't name his next asteroid after her.
He doesn't leave baskets of blueberries on her step.
He doesn't fall off his bicycle
or join up the stars to form her face.
He doesn't start blubbing. He certainly doesn't write poems.

But one evening he borrows the novel
she's always reading. Notice the spine
hidden under the stack of marking.

[47]

He hopes she doesn't. The central character's
on the run, though it's not clear from what.

Meanwhile, a reindeer's shredded in the snow
and something tracks blood
as far as the split in the telescope's fence:
attend to these portents. Vaisala doesn't.

VI

Vaisala's idea was to use a dish of mercury
as a lens and send up white
weather balloons
to give the sky scale:
many new asteroids slip in his ken,

he kisses the girl though she seems
reluctant to often repeat the experiment,
using a ballpoint
he slides the skein from his ersatz coffee.
Colleagues mention his planet is in the ascendant:

trite, clichéd and not even
astrologically true,
as strained as the proverbial thread
that's thinner by now than borscht in wartime.

VII

Here's a way to find asteroids:
shoot the sky twice with a brilliant camera
hours apart and watch
for the least significant movement
you'd still call a movement.

Like every heavenly body,
the moment's passed and all you see is the ripple:
Vitruvian Man on his back in the pool,
concentric circles still flowering
where a minute ago he twitched his arm.

Astronomers are accurate historians.
Clear nights are clocks running right
that can't tell their own time, but we can.
Even the future buzzes, under our skulls.

VIII

Another reindeer gets its bones cracked open.
Teethmarks. Something moving at high speed.
The girl won't kiss him.
Nor will she take his hand
over the mercury,

litres of which they'll find
under the floorboards years later.
He patents his weather balloons.

The old glass lens gets rolled out and left
in the snow, which is ribboning blood.

Vaisala's still stuck on the novel.
He calls his next asteroid 'Sinuhe' after the title
and isn't surprised when he sees it
change course, cut hard towards him.

IX

'She came in smiling blood.
He was marking. She took his hand
and he didn't seem to notice the blood
or say a word as she led him out . . .
They disappeared at the edge of the wood.'

'Do you know where they went?'
'No, but walking home
I saw where the snow had taken the curves
of a pair of bodies lain spreadeagled
and someone had paced a circle around each one.'

'Did you see her again?'
'He wasn't the same. Shamen, he told me,
could navigate by the sound of stars,
but she'd been his sundial's gnomon, his true North.'

X

Which wasn't the case. The bigger the lens,
the wider you'll open the past;
Vaisala had his the wrong way round
and saw the future?
Vaisala's last patent was terraforming.

In two hundred years New Finland
is either a floating archipelago
perpetually following summer, or else a 2D plane of lakes
where every lecturer has their own dacha
and perfect sunset. No specks on these photos. No dust.

'We've seen enough, Scully. Time
to make our way from these darkling academies.
Think this country does coffee?'
Missing the old lens, not quite snowed under.

Borders

For once the escalator bites its tongue.
The halogens stop flirting with the dust,
the second hand waits quietly on six,
the sliding doors are holding one long breath,
the CD racks have had their teeth pulled out,
the tills have sold themselves and disappeared,
the arphid scanners have no shoplifters
to howl against, the shuttered coffeeshop
forgets to leave crop circles on the table,
the keyhole sucks a cigarette of wind,
the tannoy chokes, the unsold atlases
fall open on a nonexistent country.

Mosquito

The locksmith nobody called out
is knelt by the homemade keyhole
working his one pick, ready to
disappear down a twist of siren.

The seamstress nobody asked for
is touching a thread to the tip
of her tongue, making her mind's
eye one with the eye of the needle.

The angel nobody prayed to
might be mistaken for a flicker
in candlelight, blur after a blink.
Has brought his own pin to dance on.

Sauna

Lie still. This is the cusp of comfortable.
One thin towel can't muffle the hot slats
and a mist is pressing on you like cement.

You've become the confluence of two rivers,
one of liquid salt and one of steam, which
blend over your bones and work them edgeless –

and the tiered box is so crisp and angular,
it carves up even light like church windows.
You lie perfectly still. You are what flows.

Learning German

-ch: Think of your teeth as the dyke along the Weser leading to the restaurant. Make your breath the freezing wind, out of the cry of seabirds take your vowel-sound, and pronounce against the cyclists in both directions.

-ö: A moan of disappointment. Imagine a waiter at the end of a long shift. He brings out your main course but he's got it all wrong. Vocalise his subconscious as he mooches back towards the kitchen, clutching ten unwanted Putenwurst, no hope now of a substantial tip.

-ü: A moan of disgust. At last the waiter re-emerges with your rump-steak, mossy to the touch and oozing clear fluid from underneath. Or is he now dreaming? Pronounce the sound he utters in his sleep.

-ä: Make your mouth the grubby flat the waiter stumbles home to. He's learning English in the evenings. The waiter is your spiritual brother. He puts on his headphones and presses play: repeat with him the 'e' sound out of 'get'.

-z: Forget about the waiter, but slowly. Focus on his eyes as his outline becomes fainter, his aspirations less realistic, his surprisingly vivid personality a blur. If those eyes had tongues, what noise would they make as they dwindled down to pupils? Perhaps a sound like tssssssss.

TENSES

I learned German fifteen years ago from a private tutor named Cheops. He was multilingual, heteroglossic, polyglottish and monosyllabic, and would chase me round the vast white drawing room screaming prepositions. I picked up almost nothing, but at the end of what was to be our final lesson, he handed me his ancient dictionary: the one with indispensable woodcuts, the one I am consulting now, at random, hoping to find some clue as to his fate. By the time my family left Leipzig and returned to England I had forgotten all the German I knew.

I am learning German since January. I have a small course Monday evening. I am learning German in a small course. Speak more slowly please. My job is electrical engineer. My hobby is to ride horse. I am learning German and my trousers are blue. Yes. They are jeans.

I will learn German so utterly it will amaze you, every hidden corner and alleyway, every restaurant (the cases, accusative, dative, are all metaphorically restaurants), every side-street and bridge and ceremonial fountain. Once I've polished off the denotations I'll begin on connotation until the whole language bristles with meaning for me, it will swallow my accent, the folk memory inside will sing for me. As we thump out stress on the desks I only pay half-attention, I am thinking about the glorious end, when I ride through your city and if you want to speak there is nowhere to hide.

Gender

das Messer

Knife is immune to gender. The slick blade slides between it. Gender is represented in my dictionary by a woodcut of a fish: the knife is slipping down the fish's seam. The word is closest of the trio to *essen*, the verb *to eat*. By its sound we deduce a serrated blade, an inadequate handle. A knife from a steakhouse, maybe, without any siblings, perhaps the piece of cutlery which rattles in the drawer at night, quite perceptibly from the upstairs bedroom?

die Gabel

Fork is female. Its trinity of roads – left indirect, direct, right indirect – all give out suddenly inside this piece of salmon I'm manoeuvring. I pay no attention to the fork itself – the word has disappeared in its own literal 'gabble', the disregarded banging of the judge's gavel, the white noise of a two-ton bag of gravel pouring off the flatbed. The sound is nonetheless angelic: it truncates Gabriel, to whom every German fork pays modest tribute.

der Löffel

Spoon is male, which suggests we're holding it the wrong way up. It is the most tedious guest at a party, echoing 'love all' or 'love hell' according to your mood; it argues with you, pleads with you, whinges through its umlaut. It will end up being hammered against the kitchen table for silence: a silence in which you will rise unsteadily, not meeting the eyes of your girlfriends' parents, and take your first treacherous steps across the virgin snowfall of a second language.

The Buried Ox

I read about the Spring Ox in a book of Finnish
rural customs: at the fade of autumn, farmers
drive a pair of stakes into the earth, the earth
their tools won't break again till nearly April.
If a cobweb stretched between them freezes
there's the ox's lined forehead, his sweat-beads.
When it falls, they say *The Spring Ox bows*
his big bull head. He means to charge. An early spring.
Which means I can imagine you as one ox-horn
and me the other, and the web of road and light
between us – soon to slip away – our shining brow.

Pheasants

The streetlights blink alive at six
pre-empting the engulfing night.
The access road is overrun

by pheasants, and the new complex
for Astrophysics isn't quite
complete – in fact, it's just begun

and rising so deep in the sticks
they're worried first-year students might
not get there before graduation.

My Raleigh Hokkaido ticks
between the birds and building site,
the places where the weeds have won,

the crossroad's buried crucifix –
although that metaphor's not right
I can't think of a better one.

Hair Cuts

Hair-drifts in barbershop corners,
flushed hairballs in the sewers,
and hair ash from cremations.

Intimations of horror:
the wigshop district in Paris,
the duvet stuffed with human hair.

Scissorblades' beard residue.
Wrong colour hair snagged in the teeth
or found on the collar.

Hair seen in dreams.
Ploughed fields of hair,
hair snarling up traffic and hair

on the tip of the tongue.
Chaste hair sprouting in seminaries.
The unheard songs of hair,

buffalo-hair in waterholes,
hair as an allegory's counterweight.
The nerveless overspill. Death's cress.

Cosmos

Trade spilt across the night. We swapped
our ermine pelts for the fermented horse-
milk we called kumis, they called kuomoss.
Too cold for dancing. Mela siphoned ash
from someone's firepit to sketch a map
of where was safe to ford the frozen river.
Our languages were halves of a split flint:
they interlocked, but barely trespassed.
Like every other year, we shared tent-space
and fed the stove and spoke alternate toasts,

and now we can't explain the strange offence
they took, how while we slept they left
and saddled shivering horses in the dark.
Next morning, hoofprints led us to a half-
healed breach between the riverbanks;
a tumble into emptiness, a stillbirth.
We felt their words unravelling from ours
and headed back to camp to find the kumis
turned, stinking of vinegar and sperm.
Poured out, it left a star-chart in the skins.

The Origin of Man

after Giacomo di Verona

In a reeking, filthy workroom
man was sculpted out of oozes
so unpleasant even I, who
sleep in shit, can't scribe their odours.
If God gave you brains, you realise
that this shanty for your soul
which for nine months was wracked by gales
rose from dirt, was built of dirt.
And then you pushed yourself, stark naked
down that burrow, slick with blood . . .

All other beasts can pay their maker:
meat or marrow, wool or leather.
Only man whose skin is worthless,
only man whose flesh is sour,
tries to pay with pus and dribble.
Just a soul, and that a shattered
bauble, leaking lies and murder.
Look in front and look behind: life
swims around you like your shadow,
here at once and gone at once.

Lace

Gap grafted onto gap
the way you might craft life in retrospect:

lace filled her eyes
as cords of smoke unbraided in bongwater.

Lies of the Land

Trim the lie and make a lawn; let it grow and make a meadow.

The horse of Truth grazes the pasture of the Lie.

Truths are stiff nubbins of bulgar wheat, chilly as flint.

A lie is a pond, and when the liar leans over he fills it with his own reflection.

A lie hangs heavy on that man, a truth hangs heavy on this one.

A liar breathes on your window and writes in the condensation.

The liar is a barber who clips Truth's beard.

Truth carries no documents and slips through borders like an exile, but a lie always has its passport in order.

In a group of ten men I counted eleven liars.

A bare lie is as good as a bare leg.

Truth needs a winter-coat.

Don't believe a word you read in the Dictionary.

Lightning Source UK Ltd.
Milton Keynes UK
UKOW04f0446230813

215840UK00004B/9/P

9 781844 719648